Five Plays for Today

TONYA TRAPPE

Level 2

Series Editors: Andy Hopkins and Jocelyn Potter

T0346366

Pearson Education Limited
Edinburgh Gate, Harlow,
Essex CM20 2JE, England
and Associated Companies throughout the world.

ISBN: 978-1-4082-2104-4

This edition first published by Pearson Education Ltd 2010

11

Text copyright © Tonya Trappe 2010
Illustrations by Tyson Smith

Set in 11/14pt Bembo
Printed in Great Britain
SWTC/06

Published by Pearson Education Ltd

Every effort has been made to trace the copyright holders and we apologise in advance
for any unintentional omissions. We would be pleased to insert the appropriate
acknowledgement in any subsequent edition of this publication.

For a complete list of the titles available in the Pearson English Readers series, please
visit www.pearsonenglishreaders.com. Alternatively, write to your local Pearson Education
office or to Pearson English Readers Marketing Department, Pearson Education,
Edinburgh Gate, Harlow, Essex CM20 2JE, England.

Contents

SUSAN	[*bored*] Yes, we know, Sam.
ANNA	It's wonderful, Sam. I'd like to …
SAM	[*not listening*] And did I tell you about my new computer? It's great. I love it.
ANNA	Is it the same as …?
SAM	[*not listening*] Look at my new jeans. They were very expensive. Do you like them?
SUSAN	[*not interested*] They're OK. You wore them yesterday.
ANNA	I think …
SAM	[*showing them his phone*] Did I show you my new phone? It takes very nice photos. Here's a photo of me on a horse! Oh, yes – and look, everybody! This is a *really* good photo of me!
PAUL	[*looking*] That's nice.
ANNA	Oh Sam, that's …
SAM	I love showing my photos to friends.
SUSAN	Yes, Sam, but you showed us those photos yesterday … [*smiling at Paul*] and the day before yesterday!
ANNA	[*taking her phone out of her bag*] I've got a photo of …
SAM	But I have some *great* photos of me … Look! In this photo I'm climbing – and I'm running in this picture. Here I am on my new motorbike and here I am … [*He continues, but nobody is listening to him.*]
PAUL	[*to Anna*] I'd like to see *your* photo, Anna. Please show me.

'Look, everybody! This is a really good photo of me!'

ANNA	It's a picture of Sam and me. We went to a party last week.
PAUL	That's a great photo of you.
ANNA	[*smiling*] Thanks!
PAUL	[*showing Sam*] Look, Sam. Isn't it great?
SAM	Oh, yes, I look good in that.
PAUL	And Anna is lovely too …

SAM   I really enjoyed that party. I love dancing. I have a
           photo of me at that party ... [*He looks at his photos.
           He is not listening.*]

SUSAN   I didn't see you at Lisa's party, Paul.

PAUL   [*shyly*] I don't really like parties.

SUSAN   Why not?

PAUL   I can't dance ... but I'd like to learn.

SUSAN   It's easy. We can teach you. We're going to another
           party tonight. Come with us!

PAUL   Really?

SUSAN   Of course.

PAUL   Thanks. I'd love to!

ANNA   [*looking at Paul's book*] Oh, that's a great book. [*She
           takes a book out of her bag.*] Do you know *this* book?

PAUL   Yes. I read it on holiday. It's great. Do *you* like reading?

ANNA   Yes, I love reading.

SUSAN   Me too.

ANNA   Sam isn't really interested in books. He prefers sport.

SAM   [*suddenly looking up*] I *love* sport. I like tennis. Look!
           [*showing a photo*] I'm playing tennis in this picture.
           I'm a good player ... [*He continues, but nobody
           is listening.*]

PAUL   [*to the girls*] Do you like sport?

ANNA AND
SUSAN   Yes, we do.

4

SUSAN	We like tennis and swimming.
ANNA	Do *you* like sport, Paul?
PAUL	I prefer to read. What other hobbies have you got?
SUSAN	I like listening to music.
PAUL	What music do you like?
SUSAN	I love dance music. Do *you* like listening to music?
PAUL	Yes, I do. And I love films and long walks in the country. And I like sitting in cafés and …
SUSAN	Let's go for a coffee now.
ANNA	Yes. Good idea. What do you think, Paul?
PAUL	Great! [*to Sam*] Are you coming? … SAM!
SAM	[*looking up from his phone*] … and here's a photo … What?
SUSAN	[*to Sam*] We're going for a coffee. [*Paul and Anna leave. Sam starts following them.*] Wait, Sam. Your friend Paul is really nice. I really like him. We had a great conversation.
SAM	A great conversation with *Paul*! [*laughing*] That's funny!
SUSAN	Why are you laughing, Sam? We really did have a nice conversation. He's fun.
SAM	What did he talk about? He hasn't got a motorbike, he doesn't play computer games. He's nice, but …
SUSAN	Stop talking, Sam, and *listen*. He asks *questions* – and he *listens* to the answers. Watch and learn from him, my friend! Then you'll be OK!

5

Let's talk now!

JUDY   EMILY

[*Judy is looking out of her bedroom window. She is sad and bored.*]

JUDY   [*looking down onto the street*] People like living in towns.
            I don't understand why. Look at those people! They are
            always running. *Always* late for something. No time for
            hobbies. No time for friends. Busy, busy, busy, all the
            time. I haven't got any friends in town. My friends are
            in the country. I love the country. I hate, hate, *hate* it
            here! I want to …

[*Emily opens the window next to Judy's and looks out.*]

EMILY   [*seeing Judy*] Judy?

JUDY   [*turning her head*] Hello, Emily.

EMILY   [*surprised*] Do you live *there*?

JUDY   Yes, I do.

EMILY   That's funny. I live at number 12 and you live at number
            14! I see you every day at school and I didn't know! Did
            you know?

JUDY   Yes, I did. I often see you in the street – and at your
            front door.

EMILY   Why didn't you tell me?

JUDY   You don't talk to me at school.

EMILY   Yes, er … I'm sorry about that. But I don't know you
            very well. And I'm always with my friends at school …
            and you are a very quiet girl. And, of course, you *are* the
            new girl.

JUDY	But I arrived when the school year started. That's more than a month!
EMILY	Oh, Judy … We didn't think. What can I say? Oh …
JUDY	It's OK. I understand. Everybody is very busy, and I'm shy, and …
EMILY	I know. Let's talk now!
JUDY	[*happily*] Great!
EMILY	[*laughing*] OK … Where did you go to school *last* year?
JUDY	I lived in a small village. I went to school there.
EMILY	Did you like it?
JUDY	[*sadly*] Yes, I did.
EMILY	But life is better in a big town. You can meet more people, make a lot of friends. You can go to cafés, watch films …
JUDY	[*very sadly*] I prefer the country. I had a lot of friends in my village. I haven't got any friends here, in town.
EMILY	But you will have. You'll see. I've got a lot of friends, and we often go out … [*trying to see into Judy's bedroom*] I like your room.
JUDY	Careful! Don't fall! Remember – we're on the 6th floor.
EMILY	[*laughing*] You're right. I forgot! [*hearing a noise inside*] Wait a minute. I'll be back. [*She goes inside, but comes back. quickly.*] Sorry, it was my cat, Charlie, at my bedroom door.
JUDY	Oh, you've got a cat! Wait there a minute. [*She goes away, then comes back with a book of photos.*] Look!

'What's this?'

EMILY   [*taking the photos*] What's this?

JUDY   Photos of my cat. He stayed in the village.

EMILY   So don't you see him now?

JUDY   Yes, when I go there at weekends.

EMILY   [*looking at the photos*] Oh, he looks lovely. Do you go *every* weekend?

JUDY   Not every weekend, but often. I visit my dad.

EMILY   I go on holidays with my dad every year. Only my mum and I live here.

JUDY   Are you sad about that?

EMILY   A little. It *was* difficult, but it's OK now.

JUDY   I understand. It *is* difficult, but it *does* get easier.

EMILY   [*hearing something*] That's my mum. I have to go now.

JUDY   [*taking her photos back*] OK. Bye.

EMILY   I'll see you tomorrow. Thanks, Judy.

JUDY   [*smiling*] See you tomorrow at school.

[*The two girls go inside. Suddenly Emily comes back.*]

EMILY   [*calling*] Judy, are you there?

JUDY   [*coming quickly to the window*] Yes?

EMILY   Do you want to walk to school with me tomorrow?

JUDY   Great!

[*The two girls go back inside. After a minute Emily comes back.*]

EMILY   [*calling*] Judy?

JUDY   [*coming to the window*] Yes?

EMILY   Em … Oh, it's OK. I'll tell you tomorrow. We'll have time.

[*They smile and close their windows.*]

9

Say it!

JANE	JANE 2, the voice in Jane's head [*speaks Jane's thoughts*]
LEO	LEO 2, the voice in Leo's head [*speaks Leo's thoughts*]

[*Jane is sitting at a bus stop. Jane 2 is standing behind her. Leo arrives He doesn't see Jane, but she sees him. He sits next to her. Leo 2 comes and stands behind Leo. When Leo 2 and Jane 2 speak, Leo and Jane's faces must show their feelings.*]

JANE 2   Leo is sitting next to me! *Leo* is sitting next to *me*! I want to talk to him, but I can't. I'm too shy.

[*Leo and Leo 2 turn their heads and see Jane.*]

LEO 2   Is that *Jane*! I sat down next to *Jane*! Oh, she's *beautiful!* I'd like to tell her, but she never speaks to me. She never *looks* at me!

[*Jane and Jane 2 look quickly at Leo.*]

JANE 2   I'd like to talk to him, but he never speaks to me He never *looks* at me!

[*Jane and Jane 2 look at Leo. Leo and Leo 2 look at Jane. They smile. They look at their feet. Jane 2 and Leo 2 look up.*]

LEO 2   She smiled at me! What can I say? … I'll say 'hello'.

LEO   [*quickly looking up*] Hello, Jane. [*He looks at his feet.*]

JANE 2   He said my name! … I must answer … Oh no – I can't speak! But I'll try. I'll say 'hi'.

JANE   [*looking up very quickly, then looking away*] Hi.

LEO 2   She hates me!

JANE 2   He thinks I'm stupid!

10

'She hates me!'   *'He thinks I'm stupid!'*

LEO 2   She thinks I'm stupid.

JANE 2   He hates me.

LEO 2   I'll say something nice. That's a good idea!

LEO   [*looking up*] What time is it?

LEO 2	Why did I say that? That's not *nice. And* I've got a watch!
JANE 2	He's bored. He wants the bus to come.
JANE	[*looking at her watch, then at Leo*] It's 5 o'clock. The bus will be here in five minutes.
LEO	Good. [*He looks at his feet.*]
LEO 2	*Good!* Why did I say 'good'? I'm stupid, stupid, *stupid!*
JANE	Sometimes it comes early.
LEO 2	She's bored. She hopes it will come early today!
JANE	And sometimes it's late.
JANE 2	Why can't I stop talking! 'Sometimes it's early, sometimes it's late.' That's *really* interesting!
LEO	Good.
LEO 2	'Good' *again!* Stop talking, Leo, *stop talking!*
JANE 2	He *hates* me.
LEO 2	I'll try again.
LEO	[*quietly*] I like your jacket.
JANE 2	What did he say?
JANE	Pardon?
LEO	[*a little louder*] I like your jacket.
JANE	Thanks. [*She smiles at him.*] I like your T-shirt.
LEO	Thanks. I like yours
JANE 2	[*after a short time*] I think he likes me!
LEO 2	I think she likes me! I'll try again.

LEO   I like your shoes.

JANE   [*laughing*] Thanks. ... I like your jacket.

LEO   Thanks.

LEO 2   I'm talking to Jane! *I* am talking to *Jane*!

JANE 2   He really does like me!

LEO 2   She really does like me!

JANE 2   Perhaps he only likes my clothes.

LEO   Jane ...

JANE 2   He said my name again!

LEO   I like, I like ...

JANE 2   What? What do you like? You can say it!

LEO   I like ...

JANE 2   Say it, Leo! Don't be shy.

LEO   I like ... *you*. I like you very much.

LEO 2   Oh no. Why did I say that? What's she going to say?

JANE 2   *YES*!

JANE   I really like you too, Leo.

Young love!

| SUE | DANNY | ALEX | JOHN |
| WAITER | MAN | WOMAN | |

[*Sue is sitting in a café. A man and a woman are sitting at a different table. They are older than Sue. The man is reading a newspaper. A waiter is speaking to Sue. The woman is listening.*]

WAITER   Can I get you anything?

SUE   No, thank you. I'm waiting for my boyfriend.

WOMAN   [*to the man*] Young love! That's nice.

MAN   [*looking up from his newspaper*] Yes, but the boy is late.

WOMAN   I hope he's nice.

MAN   *I* hope he's *quiet*. I want to read my newspaper!

[*Danny comes in and looks round the café. He sees Sue.*]

DANNY   [*to Sue, shouting angrily*] Where *were* you yesterday? I waited for hours!

SUE   [*shouting back*] What are you talking about?

MAN   Shh. Can you speak more quietly, please!

WOMAN   We're trying to have a *quiet* cup of tea!

DANNY   [*to Sue, quietly but angrily*] Why didn't you meet me yesterday? Were you with another guy?

SUE   No! Of course not!

DANNY   So where were you?

SUE   Em ... em ... I was at my grandmother's house. [*sadly*] She's very ill.

14

'Where were you yesterday? I waited for hours!'

DANNY	Oh! I'm sorry.
SUE	I really like you, Danny. You *know* that.
DANNY	I'm really very sorry, Sue. I'll never shout again.
SUE	Really? … OK.

15

DANNY	Am I the only guy in your life?
SUE	You are, Danny.
DANNY	[*smiling*] Thank you, Sue. I'm sorry, I was stupid.
MAN	[*to the woman*] What do you think? Is she lying?
WOMAN	Of course not.
MAN	Don't be stupid. Of course she is.
WOMAN	Let's listen to the conversation. You'll see.
MAN	[*putting down the newspaper*] *You'll* see. I'm right! She's got *two* boyfriends.
WAITER	[*to Danny and Sue*] Can I get you anything?
DANNY	Yes please, a coffee.
SUE	A glass of water. [*to Danny*] Sorry. I haven't got any money.
WAITER	[*quietly to the other customers*] She *never* has any!
DANNY	*I've* got money, Sue. Have something.
SUE	Thanks. [*to the waiter*] A coffee too, please.
WAITER	OK. [*He sees Alex outside and speaks quietly to the man and the woman.*] Watch this. It will be very interesting!

[*Alex comes in and looks round the cafe. The waiter and the man watch him, interested. The woman is listening to Sue and Danny.*]

DANNY	You are wonderful, Sue.
SUE	You too, Danny.
WOMAN	[*to the man*] They're in love. *She* hasn't got two boyfriends.

16

'Hi, Sue. This is a nice surprise!'

MAN   You'll see!

[*Alex sees Sue. He is surprised and happy.*]

ALEX   Hi, Sue. This is a nice surprise! [*to Danny*] Hi, I'm Alex. [*He sits down.*]

DANNY   [*not happy*] Hi, I'm Danny.

ALEX   [*to Sue*] What are you doing here? Why aren't you at your grandmother's house?

DANNY   [*but Alex is not listening*] That was yesterday.

17

SUE	[*standing up*] Yes. We're going there now. [*pulling Danny's arm*] Let's go, Danny. We're late. Sorry, Alex. See you later. We really must go now!
WAITER	[*putting the drinks on the table*] Two coffees.
ALEX	Then why have you got coffees?
DANNY	[*not understanding*] Sit down, Sue. Drink your coffee.
ALEX	[*to the waiter*] A coffee for me too, please. [*to Danny*] Do you know Sue's grandmother?

[*Danny and Sue talk at the same time.*]

DANNY	No, I don't.
SUE	Yes, he does. I mean ... I mean ... [*speaking very quickly*] Alex, do you like this café? *I* like this café ... I come here often because I like the coffee here ... It's fun here. I like the people ...
ALEX	Stop talking, Sue. I want to ask you a question.
DANNY	[*starting to understand*] Me too. I have a question for you.

[*Sue, Alex and Danny talk at the same time.*]

ALEX	[*to Sue, talking about Danny*] Who *is* this guy?
DANNY	[*to Sue*] Were you with *Alex* yesterday?
SUE	It's very hot in here. I must ... [*Suddenly she hears her phone. They all stop talking. She answers it. She gets up and walks quickly away from the table*] Hello? Hello?
MAN	[*happily, to the woman*] Now what do you think?
WOMAN	Oh dear! Perhaps she *has* got two boyfriends.

WAITER	[*listening to their conversation*] No, she hasn't!
MAN	[*to the waiter*] Of course she has.
WOMAN	Perhaps you *are* right.
MAN	I'm *always* right!
WAITER	[*smiling happily*] We'll see.

[*Sue is talking on the phone. She is now standing next to the man and the woman's table. Danny and Alex are talking angrily.*]

| SUE | Sorry – *who* is it? John! Oh no! ... What? ... *Did* I say 'oh no'? ... Of course I want to speak to you, John. ... Yes, I *am* in the café. ... No! Please don't come. ... Because I'm leaving now. ... Why am I leaving? Er ... because I don't like the people here. They aren't very nice. No, *really* John, the people in the café today are ... John? John? Are you there? ... He didn't say goodbye! |

[*The man and the woman look angrily at Sue.*]

SUE	[*seeing their faces*] Oh, I'm sorry. It's not *you*! *You're* very nice, but I've got a problem. I'm really sorry. Can I buy you a drink?
MAN	[*calling to the waiter*] A bottle of red wine, please.
SUE	A bottle!
WOMAN	Can I ask you a question?
SUE	[*sitting down at their table*] Yes?
WOMAN	[*very quietly*] Have you got two boyfriends?
SUE	[*very quietly*] No, I haven't. I've got ...

WOMAN   [*to the man*] You heard her. *I* was right. She *hasn't* got two boyfriends.

[*John comes in and looks round the café. He sees Sue with the man and the woman. He sees Danny and Alex fighting.*]

JOHN   [*to Sue*] Oh, yes. You were right. Those boys really *aren't* very nice.

SUE   [*standing up*] Yes, let's go – quickly.

DANNY   [*calling, angrily*] Sue! Which of us is your boyfriend?

JOHN   [*to Sue*] Do you *know* them? [*calling to the other boys*] *I* am.

DANNY AND
ALEX   *You* are!

WAITER   [*loudly, to everybody*] She has *three* boyfriends!

THE BOYS   She has *what?*

MAN   [*happily*] I was right!

WOMAN   [*to the man*] No, *I* was right! She *hasn't* got two. She's got *three!*

SUE   [*to Danny*] But I like you [*to John*] and you [*to Alex*] and you. What can I do?

THE BOYS   [*shouting*] BUT WHICH OF US IS YOUR *BOYFRIEND?*

SUE   Er … er … [*to Danny*] You?

DANNY   No, thank you! [*He leaves.*]

SUE   [*smiling at Alex*] I prefer you to him.

ALEX   I'm not stupid, Sue! [*He leaves.*]

20

SUE   [*to John*] You win! I like you the best!

JOHN   Goodbye! I hope that I never see you again! [*He leaves.*]

MAN AND
WOMAN   [*leaving, to Sue*] Goodbye, and thanks! We had fun
           here today.

WAITER   [*to Sue*] Three coffees and a bottle of wine. Twenty
           pounds, please.

SUE   [*taking a lot of money out of her bag*] I'll never have
           more than one boyfriend again! It's very expensive!

'BUT WHICH OF US IS YOUR BOYFRIEND?'

We're not going away!

THREE GIRL BULLIES	OLIVER	SALLY
THREE BOY BULLIES	OLIVER'S MOTHER	JEFF
THE HEAD TEACHER	AN OLD WOMAN	

[*On the left, we can see bullies outside a school. In the middle, Oliver's mother is reading in her living room. On the right, the head teacher is working at a desk.*]

ALL BULLIES We are a gang of bullies.

BULLY 1 [*kicking and pushing other bullies*] We are very LOUD and bad.

BULLY 2 [*enjoying the word*] Bad, bad, *bad*.

BULLY 3 Really, *really* BAD.

BULLY 1 We're big and strong and we're never ... uh? ... uh?

BULLY 5 Wrong!

BULLY 4 Right!

[*They all laugh stupidly.*]

BULLY 5 [*surprised*] We're never *right*?

BULLY 4 No, stupid! I mean ... That's *right* – we're never *wrong*!

BULLY 5 [*kicking the ground, then pushing Bully 4*] I'm not stupid!

BULLY 1 We're very *intelligent*! [*shouting*] OK?

BULLY 5 Yes we're very intelli ... intelli ... intelligiment.

BULLY 3 [*pushing Bully 5*] *Intelligent*, stupid!

BULLY 5 [*pushing Bully 3*] I'm not stupid – *you're* stupid!

22

| BULLY 1 | We are famous in this town. |
| BULLY 6 | When you're up, we'll bring you down! |

[*They all laugh.*]

BULLY 4	We are not afraid of anybody.
BULLY 6	Nobody.
BULLY 5	We're big and strong and never … uh? …
BULLY 4	WRONG! [*quietly, about Bully 5*] Stupid.
BULLY 1	[*loudly*] We're going to stay,
BULLY 3	We're not going away. [*to Bully 5*] OK?
BULLY 5	[*angrily*] OK. I'm not stupid. We're going to stay.

'We're not going away.'

23

BULLY 1   WE … ARE … NOT … GOING … AWAY!

ALL BULLIES   O … K.

[*They all laugh loudly and stupidly.*]

BULLY 1   BECAUSE   WE'RE   NOT   AFRAID   OF
          ANYBODY!

ALL BULLIES   NOBODY!

[*They all laugh stupidly.*]

BULLY 1   [*loudly*] And who is the boss?

ALL BULLIES   [*quietly*] *You* are the boss.

BULLY 1   And why?

BULLIES   Because you're not afraid of anybody!

BULLY 1   Good.

[*The head teacher comes out of her office. She looks at the bullies. They look back. She is angry, but she doesn't speak. She goes back into her office.*]

HEAD   [*sadly*] I must do something. They *are* a big problem.

BULLY 1   What did *she* want?

BULLY 2   She's stupid.

BULLY 3   She's afraid.

BULLY 4   I hate that head teacher.

BULLY 5   I hate school.

BULLY 6   I hate everybody.

[*An old woman arrives. She is carrying a heavy bag.*]

24

BULLY 1   Look! An old woman. Let's have some fun!

[*They all laugh.*]

BULLY 1   Hello. Is that bag heavy?

OLD WOMAN   [*thinking that the bully will carry it*] Thank you Yes.

BULLIES   Good!

[*They all laugh and push the old woman onto the ground. The old woman looks afraid and gets up quickly. Then she leaves as quickly as she can. Oliver arrives.*]

BULLY 1   Hi, Oliver.

'Hi, Oliver.'

OLIVER	[*afraid*] What do you want?
BULLY 2	Are you afraid?

[*The bullies laugh stupidly.*]

OLIVER	Yes … I am.
BULLIES	Good! [*They push Oliver.*]
BULLY 3	Have you got any money?
OLIVER	No, I haven't.
BULLY 2	Go home. Get some money. We'll wait here.

[*They all laugh.*]

OLIVER	But I haven't got any money.
BULLY 4	Go and ask your mother. *She* has money.
BULLY 5	And come back quickly!

[*Oliver runs to the living room. The bullies and the head teacher watch Oliver's conversation with his mother.*]

MOTHER	Hello, Oliver. How was your day at school?
OLIVER	Hi, Mum. It was OK. [*He sits down and looks at his feet.*]
MOTHER	Is everything OK, Oliver?
OLIVER	Yes … no. I mean … yes, I'm fine.
MOTHER	Is there a problem? Tell me, Oliver.
BULLIES	Don't tell her, Oliver!
OLIVER	I can't tell you.
BULLIES	[*laughing*] Good. He's afraid of us. He won't tell her.

MOTHER	Oliver, you must tell me. Perhaps I can help.
OLIVER	[*quietly*] Nobody can help.
MOTHER	Is there a problem at school?
OLIVER	Mum, please. Forget it. There isn't a problem. OK?
MOTHER	OK, Oliver. But you can tell me your problems. You know that.
OLIVER	Mum … I *must* have some money.
MUM	What did you do with your pocket money?
BULLIES	Don't tell her, Oliver!
OLIVER	I bought some music.
MOTHER	I'm not going to give you more money Oliver. You'll have to wait for next month's pocket money.
OLIVER	But Mum …
MOTHER	[*leaving the room*] OLIVER! I said NO!
BULLIES	Take some money, Oliver. Take it from her bag.
HEAD	[*sadly*] Don't take money, Oliver. Don't take your mother's money.
BULLIES	TAKE IT!
HEAD	DON'T TAKE IT!

[*Oliver quickly opens his mother's bag. He takes some money and goes back to the bullies.*]

HEAD	Oh, no. What can I do? We must stop this.
BULLY 1	[*taking the money*] Good, Oliver.

BULLY 6	We'll be back tomorrow.
BULLY 5	Have more money ready for us.

[*They laugh stupidly and loudly. They leave. Jeff and Sally arrive. The bullies push and kick them. Jeff and Sally run to Oliver. Oliver is sitting down in the street with his head in his hands. The bullies walk away.*]

JEFF	Hi, Oliver. Are you OK?
SALLY	Oliver. Is there a problem?
OLIVER	[*sadly*] No, I'm fine. Really.
JEFF	Oliver, you can talk to your friends. What's wrong?
OLIVER	I'm a bad person.
SALLY	You're *not* a bad person, Oliver!
OLIVER	Yes, I am. I lied to my mother and I took money from her bag!

[*Jeff, Sally and Oliver continue talking. Oliver's mother comes back into the living room and looks in her bag. She suddenly looks surprised. She makes a phone call and the head teacher answers her phone. They speak quietly. They say goodbye and Oliver's mother goes to the head teacher's office.*]

JEFF	You too! *I* took money from my mother's bag *yesterday*.
SALLY	For the bullies?
OLIVER	Yes.
JEFF	You too, Sally?
SALLY	Yes. But I was afraid.
JEFF	Me too.

OLIVER   This isn't going to stop. We have to tell somebody.

SALLY   You're right. We can't take money every day.

JEFF   But what are our parents going to say. We took their money!

SALLY   Perhaps they'll understand. We didn't *want* to take it.

OLIVER   We were afraid of the bullies.

SALLY   Let's talk to the head teacher.

OLIVER   What can she do?

SALLY   I don't know. Perhaps together we can think of something.

JEFF   OK. We must talk to somebody. Let's go.

[*They go to the head teacher's office. She is with Oliver's mother now.*]

OLIVER   Mum! What are you doing here?

MOTHER   The head teacher told me about the bullies.

SALLY   [*to the head teacher*] You knew about them?

HEAD   Yes, but the problem is worse than I thought.

OLIVER   I'm sorry, Mum, but I gave them your money.

MOTHER   Why didn't you tell me about the bullies?

OLIVER   I don't know … I was afraid of them. I'm sorry.

MOTHER   [*to the head teacher*] What can we do?

HEAD   There isn't an easy answer.

OLIVER   We can find an answer. Together we can stop them. They're stupid!

29

'They're stupid, but they're dangerous.'

HEAD   They're stupid, but they're dangerous.

MOTHER   Can't we phone the police?

HEAD   Yes we can, but will that stop the bullies?

MOTHER   Perhaps they will be afraid of the police.

HEAD   We can try.

JEFF   We *must* do something!

[*The bullies come back. They are angry and they are shouting. The other people watch, afraid.*]

BULLIES   We're a gang of bullies.

             We're very loud and bad.

We're big and strong

And we're never wrong.

WE'RE NOT AFRAID OF ANYBODY.

We are famous in this town.

When you're up, we'll bring you down.

We'll fight you and we'll kick you.

WE'RE NOT AFRAID OF ANYBODY.

We're not going away.

We *are* going to stay – and

WE'RE NOT AFRAID OF ANYBODY.

MOTHER   [*to the head teacher*] Call the police!

BULLIES   WE'RE NOT AFRAID OF ANYBODY.

HEAD   OK, I will. But will that stop them?

BULLIES   WE'RE NOT AFRAID OF ANYBODY.

JEFF AND
SALLY   We must find an answer to this problem.

BULLIES   WE'RE NOT GOING AWAY!

OLIVER   It isn't going to be easy, but we must try.

BULLIES   WE'RE NOT AFRAID OF ANYBODY.

MOTHER   The police will find an answer.

OLIVER   I hope you're right, Mum. Imagine life without them.

BULLIES   WE'RE NOT GOING AWAY!

ACTIVITIES

Watch and learn!

Before you read

1 Read the Introduction to this book. Are these sentences about the first play right or wrong?

  a Paul is shy.

  b Sam asks a lot of questions.

  c Paul doesn't stop talking.

  d The girls answer Paul's questions.

  e Sam listens to the answers.

2 Find these words in the Word List at the back of the book. Then use them in these sentences.

act fun hobbies imagine play prefer shy surprised

Every year our school does a **(a)** ..... in the school theatre. I like to **(b)** ..... in it. I have other **(c)** ..... too. I like tennis and football but I **(d)** ..... tennis to football. But the best **(e)** ..... is in the school theatre when we do the play. The first time, I was a little **(f)** ..... . I didn't want to be in it. But now I can't **(g)** ..... my life without the theatre. I sang a song in the play this year. My parents were very **(h)** ..... because I never sing at home.

While you read

3 Write the name/names in these sentences

  a .... talks about computer games and sports.

  b .... has a new motorbike.

  c .... like tennis and swimming.

  d .... can't dance.

  e .... are going to a party tonight.

  f .... like listening to music.

  g .... likes sitting in cafés.

  h .... doesn't play computer games.

After you read

4 Talk to other students.

  a Talk about your hobbies. What do you like doing?

  b Which boy do you prefer: Paul or Sam? Why?

Let's talk now! and **Say it!**

Before you read

5 Talk to other students. Which do you prefer: the country or the town? Why?

While you read

6 <u>Underline</u> the one wrong word in each of these sentences. Write the right word

   a Judy loves living in the town. ....
   b Emily thinks that life is worse in a big town. ....
   c Judy has a lot of friends. ....
   d Emily goes on holiday with her mum every year. ....
   e Emily has a dog. ....
   f Judy lives with her dad. ....

7 Make sentences

   a Jane 2   says 'hello' first.
   b Leo 2   are waiting at a bus stop.
   c Leo and Jane   speaks Leo's thoughts.
   d Jane   speaks Jane's thoughts.
   e Leo   says 'hi'.

After you read

8 Work with another student.

   a What will Emily tell Judy the next day on the way to school? Discuss this, and then have the conversation.
   b Imagine Leo and Jane's next conversation. What will they talk about? Have the conversation.

9 Which people in these two plays are shy? How is life difficult for them? How can they – and other people – make it easier?

Young love!

Before you read

10 Look at the picture on page 15. Who and what can you see in the picture? What is happening?

11 These people arrive at the café. Who arrives first? And then? Number them 1–4.

John ..... Danny ..... Sue ..... Alex .....

After you read

12 Which sentences are right?

    a Danny is angry when he arrives at the café.

    b Sue lies to him about her grandmother.

    c Danny knows when Sue is lying.

    d Sue always pays for her drinks.

    e Alex comes to the café because Sue is there.

    f John comes to the café because Sue is there.

    g Sue has got two boyfriends.

    h The waiter and the other two customers enjoy their time in the café.

13 Discuss these questions with other students.

    a Sue had three boyfriends. Is that a good idea? Why (not)?

    b Who do you like best in the play? Why?

We're not going away!

Before you read

14 Think about the name of the play and look at the people in the picture on page 23. What do you think is going to happen in this play?

While you read

15 <u>Underline</u> the best word in *italics*.

    a The bullies are very *loud / quiet*.

    b The head teacher *is doing / wants to do* something about the bullies.

    c The old woman arrives *before / after* Oliver.

    d The bullies want *Oliver's money / to kill Oliver.*

    e The bullies *can / can't* hear the conversation between Oliver and his mother.

    f Oliver tells his mother *lies / everything.*

    g Sally and Jeff are friends of *the bullies / Oliver.*

    h Sally and Jeff are *not / also* afraid of the bullies.

i *Oliver / The head teacher* tells Oliver's mother about the problem.

j Oliver *hopes / thinks* that the police will find an answer.

After you read

16 Bullies can be a problem at work or at school. Discuss these questions with other students.

    a Do you have this problem, or did you in the past? What are you doing/did you do about it?

    b Do you know any bullies, or were you one? Why are people bullies?

    c What is the best answer to Oliver's problem?

Writing

17 Write about your hobbies. What do you like doing with and without your friends?

18 Write three good things and three bad things about life in the town and life in the country. Which do you prefer? Why?

19 Leo and Jane continue their conversation. They are excited and happy. Now they can talk about their feelings! Write the conversation.

20 Write about Sue ('Young love!'). Imagine her everyday life. Why do you think she plays games with young men?

21 The bullies *are* afraid of the police. They stop asking for money. But the problem starts again. Oliver's mother writes a letter to a newspaper about the problem. She tells Oliver's story from start to finish. Write her letter. You can start like this:

Dear Sir/Madam,

There is a big problem in our town. Parents must talk to their children about it. This happened to my son and his friends …

22 Which play did you like reading or acting best? Why? Write about it.